DREAM JOBS
If You Like

FOOD

by Amie Jane Leavitt

CAPSTONE PRESS

a capstone imprint

Capstone Captivate is published by Capstone Press, an imprint of Capstone.
1710 Roe Crest Drive
North Mankato, Minnesota 56003
www.capstonepub.com

Library of Congress Cataloging-in-Publication Data is available on the Library of Congress website.
ISBN: 978-1-4966-8396-0 (library binding)
ISBN: 978-1-4966-8447-9 (eBook PDF)

Summary: Wouldn't it be cool to have a job working with or around the things you love? Do you like decorating cupcakes? Maybe a career as a cake decorator would be a sweet gig! Readers will discover the possibilities of careers working with food.

Image Credits
iStockphoto: andresr, 22, CentralITAlliance, 10, EduardSV, 13, SDI Productions, 21, tdub303, 4; Newscom: Adam Harnett/ZUMAPRESS, 29; Shutterstock: B Brown, 17, bondvit, 20, Craig Zerbe, 14, Darryl Brooks, 7, InaKos, (food) Cover, Juice Flair, 16, Kristi Blokhin, 23, LightField Studios, 18, MIKHAIL GRACHIKOV, (dots) design element throughout, New Africa, 8, Odua Images, back cover, 25, Rawpixel.com, 9, SFROLOV, Cover, sherwood, 15, Supavadee butradee, 26

Editorial Credits
Editor: Heather Williams; Designer: Sara Radka; Media Researcher: Morgan Walters; Production Specialist: Spencer Rosio

All internet sites appearing in back matter were available and accurate when this book was sent to press.

Printed in the United States
PA117

Table of Contents

Words in **bold** are in the glossary.

There are many jobs in the world, but only a few are dream jobs. A dream job might not make you rich or famous. But you'll be excited to go to work every day. If you love trying new foods, baking cookies, or making up recipes, one of these might be your dream job!

Baker

Many people like making cookies and cakes. They enjoy making pies and breads too. These people would enjoy a career as a baker.

Bakers use large ovens to make a variety of bread and pastries each day.

On the Job

Many people like baked goods first thing in the morning. Bakers often have to get up before sunrise. They mix up batches of bread. They drop donut rings into hot oil. And they frost cinnamon rolls. Many bakers are done with their daily baking by midmorning. They may make other baked items later in the day for special orders. When they are not baking, they are preparing and cleaning for the next day or helping customers.

FUN FACT

The world's largest wedding cake was baked in 2004 in Connecticut. It weighed 7.5 tons (6.8 metric tons). That's as much as 10 cows! The cake was made with 5 tons (4.5 t) of cake batter.

Pay Range

Average salary = $25,000 per year.

Education and Skills

People who wish to become bakers can go to **culinary** school. Many also learn on the job. Bakers should have experience in the kitchen or be willing to learn. They must know how to follow recipes and use kitchen tools. Having an imagination helps bakers make food that looks beautiful. A good baker also knows which ingredients go best together.

Food Truck Owner

Traveling restaurants called food trucks fill the streets. You can often find them parked in big cities. They also go to special events such as concerts and fairs. Food trucks sell just about any kind of food, from ice cream to fried fish.

On the Job

The world of food trucks can be tough. Food truck owners must offer creative menus. First they come up with a unique idea. Then they buy a truck. They apply for a license or permit with their city so they can open up a business. Then they fill the inside of the truck with tools to make the food. Many food trucks use social media. They post where they will be parked for the day.

Pay Range

Salary varies. Some food truck owners can sell as much as $200,000 worth of food per year. It isn't all **profit**, though. Owners must pay all of their expenses, such as gasoline and food supplies, out of that money.

Education and Skills

College is not needed. However, a degree from a culinary school may be helpful. Food truck owners should know how to make food. They are **entrepreneurs**. They have to budget money and manage workers. Food truck owners should be creative. They have to get customers in whatever way they can. Many food truck owners work inside the truck when their business is new. They cook food and serve customers. Later they may hire others to run the food truck for them.

Food trucks are small traveling restaurants that bring food to people at parks, festivals, and concerts.

Food stylists use backgrounds, props, and lighting to make food look delicious and ready to eat.

Food Stylist

Food is often pictured in magazines. Beautiful meals appear on TV and in movies. These are not just quick snapshots. They are works of art. Each one has been carefully set up by a food stylist.

On the Job

Food stylists are magicians and artists. They use many tricks to make food look perfect. For example, a plate of pancakes with maple syrup isn't what you think. The pancakes might be real. But the syrup is really motor oil! Maple syrup is very light and thin. It doesn't show up well in a photo. Food stylists paint, spray, and even add wax to food to make it look perfect. Sometimes the food stylist is also the photographer.

Food magazines and recipe websites use food stylists for perfect shots of meals and ingredients.

Pay Range

Between $30,000 and $50,000 (or more) per year.

Education and Skills

A degree in photography is helpful. People who want to become food stylists can learn many skills in classes or online. They can also work as an assistant to an experienced food stylist. This helps them learn the tricks of the trade. Food stylists should have a great **portfolio** of all the food they have set up.

Using a recipe can help you make sure your meal tastes the same each time you make it.

Recipe Writer

Recipes tell bakers and cooks how to make food in a certain way. Without a recipe, it would be tough to make the same food twice. You can find recipes in magazines, cookbooks, newspapers, and online. Recipe writers are the people who make these instructions.

On the Job

All recipes have rules, such as oven temperatures and baking times. Recipe writers must follow these rules when writing recipes. They should already know how to bake and cook. That way, they will know what kinds of instructions to give in the recipe. Recipe writers must try out their ideas. They play with ingredients. They see what tastes best together. They find ways to make recipes healthier by cutting sugar and fat. Recipe writers use a lot of trial and error.

Pay Range

Average salary = $60,000 per year.

Education and Skills

Some recipe writers go to culinary school. Some take online courses. Many learn about food on the job. They work at restaurants, **catering** companies, and bakeries. Recipe writers should write clearly and have strong math skills. Cooking and baking use a lot of math. Recipe writers should also have a good sense of taste.

FUN FACT

Ruth Graves Wakefield invented the chocolate-chip cookie in 1937. It is the most popular cookie in the United States. A poll in 2017 showed that 53 percent of Americans said chocolate-chip was their favorite.

Food Forager

Chefs buy eggs, cheeses, meats, and milk from farmers. They also like to buy ingredients that are unique and harder to find. Some of these items include wild mushrooms, dandelions, and huckleberries. These things are not sold in stores. Chefs must buy them from food foragers.

On the Job

Food foragers spend much of their day in nature. They search through forests, hillsides, and fields. Foragers keep their eyes open for **edible** ingredients. Many plants, fruits, and mushrooms can be eaten. These things can be hard to find. Foragers must pay attention to their surroundings. They must also make sure what they pick is safe to eat. Some poisonous plants look the same as safe plants. Foragers sell their items to chefs. The chefs then include these fresh ingredients in the day's menu.

Pay Range

Salary varies, since most food foragers are entrepreneurs. Some can make as much as $300 per hour on a good day.

Education and Skills

Food foragers must know which wild plants are safe and which are not. They can learn this information from books. They might also take college classes. They can even learn from another forager. Foragers must be outgoing. They need to build relationships with chefs and other food foragers in their area. Foragers are not afraid to get dirty. They must also be physically fit. Their job requires a lot of hiking.

Edible mushrooms can be tough to spot if you don't know what to look for.

Cattle are a common animal raised by ranchers.

Rancher

Ranchers raise herds of animals. The animals are raised to provide food products for people. Meat and dairy companies buy the animals from ranchers.

On the Job

Ranchers spend a lot of their time outside. Most raise cows or sheep. But some ranchers raise ostriches, emus, bison, or alpacas. Ranchers move their animals from place to place. This way, the animals have enough food and water. Ranchers take care of young animals and females about to give birth. They make sure their animals are safe from wild animals. Ranchers give their animals medicine to keep them healthy. They brand or tag them in case they get lost.

Pay Range

Average salary = $40,000 per year.

Education and Skills

Many modern ranchers get a degree in ranch management. This takes around two years. Some get degrees in **agriculture**. But not all ranchers go to college. Some learn from other ranchers. Many are born into the business. Ranchers must enjoy caring for animals. They must also be able to train animals. They often use horses and dogs to help them move their herds. Ranchers are strong and fit. They start work before the sun rises and often work until dark. Ranchers must be organized. They should be good with machinery and enjoy solving problems.

FUN FACT

Cows are ruminants. This means their stomachs have three or four different parts, and each part does a different job. Ruminants chew their food twice to soften it.

Ranchers cover a lot of ground every day, so they ride horses to save time.

Farmer

The grocery store is filled with many items. Most of them come from farmers. Farmers grow and raise most of the food we eat.

On the Job

Farmers often work from sunup to sundown. Their animals have to be fed, milked, and cared for. Some farmers raise chickens, turkeys, or dairy cows. Others raise goats or sheep. Farmers also work in fields and grow crops. Their fields need to be planted with seeds in the spring. They need to be weeded and watered all through the summer. And they need to be harvested in the fall.

Large machines, such as combine harvesters, help farmers do their jobs faster.

The fruits and vegetables sold in stores are grown on farms all across the country and around the world.

Pay Range

Varies by region. Average salary is about $69,000 per year, although some farmers make much less, and some make more. A farmer's income can change from year to year.

Education and Skills

Some farmers find it helpful to get a degree in agriculture. Others take farming classes in high school or college. Most learn on the job. Some grew up on farms and learned the business from their parents. Others worked as an **apprentice**, farm hand, or field hand. Farmers must know how to budget their money. They have to take care of machinery and repair the many buildings on the farm.

Chef

Chefs prepare food for people. There are many types of chefs. A grill chef grills meat and vegetables. A saucier makes the sauces. A pastry chef makes the desserts. Executive chefs are the masters of the kitchen. They come up with the dishes that are served. They also manage the other chefs.

Chefs are creative people who come up with unique and tasty meals for restaurants.

On the Job

Chefs have a fast-paced job. Many orders often come in at once. Orders must be made quickly. Some smaller restaurants have just one or two chefs who do all the cooking. Larger restaurants have a team. Chefs cut up ingredients. They whip up the sauces. They slice up the meat. All of these ingredients go into the final recipe. It is often a delicious work of art.

FUN FACT

Chefs often wear tall white hats called toques. Want to know who is in charge of the kitchen? Look for the chef in the tallest hat. It's always worn by the executive chef. The shorter hats are worn by the lower-ranking chefs.

Pay Range

Between $58,000 and $83,000 per year for an executive chef.

Education and Skills

Many chefs have a degree from culinary school. Other chefs learn on the job. All chefs have some skills in common. They can work in a fast-paced environment. They can keep their work space clean. And they are creative. They make each dish look nice on the plate. They must also have a good sense of taste. Chefs know that cooking is both an art and a science.

A proper diet includes just the right amounts of vitamins and minerals each day.

Dietician

Proper nutrition is important for good health. The right diet makes people feel better. It helps them be more physically active. Dieticians are the people who know the best foods to eat.

On the Job

Dieticians usually work with one client at a time. First a dietician talks with the client and reviews notes from the client's doctor. Then the dietician makes an eating plan. There are many reasons someone might need an eating plan. Some people have food allergies. Others have a health condition, such as diabetes or high blood pressure. They could be recovering from surgery or need to lose weight. The client checks in after the plan has been made. The dietician then makes any adjustments to the plan.

Pay Range

Average salary = $60,000 per year.

Education and Skills

Dieticians need a four-year college degree. They study food or nutrition science. Most dieticians complete an **internship** at a school or hospital. They work with another dietician. They get experience and learn new skills. They must be comfortable talking with people. Dieticians must be good problem-solvers. They have to find a solution for each client.

FUN FACT

Eight foods cause about 90 percent of food allergy reactions. These foods are milk, eggs, peanuts, tree nuts, wheat, soy, fish, and shellfish. Many children outgrow allergies to milk, eggs, wheat, and soy. But nut and fish allergies tend to last a lifetime.

Dieticians help schools create menus that keep kids healthy and give them energy to learn.

Restaurant Owner

Think about all the restaurants where you live. Your town might have fast-food restaurants and diners. It might have cafés and coffee shops too. All of these restaurants are owned by someone.

On the Job

Restaurant owners have many different jobs. They are often in charge of the business part of the restaurant. They must also pay for advertising, buy ingredients, and hire workers. They might also make the restaurant's menu. Restaurant owners have to make sure the restaurant is clean. They manage the chefs and servers.

Running a restaurant requires lots of organization and input from everyone, from waitstaff to cooks.

Restaurants are a big part of the culture of big cities and small towns everywhere.

Pay Range

Between $29,000 and $153,000 per year, depending on the size and success of the restaurant.

Education and Skills

Not all restaurant owners go to college. But having some kind of business training is helpful. Having experience in the food industry is also useful. Someone who has worked as a server or cook will be a step ahead of someone who hasn't. Restaurant owners must be able to work under pressure. They will have to work hard and be patient. They will also need to have money saved to pay bills when times are slow.

FUN FACT

Restaurants can be found almost anywhere. The Ithaa Undersea Restaurant is in the Maldives, a group of islands in the Indian Ocean. This dining spot is under the ocean! It is 16 feet (5 meters) below sea level. It has walls and ceilings made of glass so you can see the fish swimming by as you eat.

Food Entrepreneur

Some people love to cook. But they don't want to work in a bakery or restaurant. Instead they cook up their recipes and sell them on their own. They like to be their own boss.

On the Job

Food entrepreneurs make and sell special food items. They might have just one. Or they might offer many items. Some food entrepreneurs make baked goods. They decorate birthday and wedding cakes for customers. Others mix up spices that can be used for meats and vegetables. They put them in bottles and sell them at fairs or online. Food entrepreneurs can work from home. They can work at a rented kitchen space. They can also work at farmers' markets or travel to food festivals.

Pay Range

Average salary = $68,000 per year.

FUN FACT

Some food entrepreneurs focus on food for four-legged friends. They make dog biscuits and jerky treats. They grow chemical-free catnip. They make seed wreaths for birds and even cookies for horses.

Education and Skills

Food entrepreneurs do not have to go to college. They can simply sell a food item they love making. But many food entrepreneurs take food-prep classes. They may read books on how to run a business. They may even ask other business owners for advice. It is cool to be your own boss. But it can also be risky. You are responsible for every part of the process. Having job freedom requires a lot of responsibility.

Food entrepreneurs can often be found selling their freshly made cakes or doughnuts at parks or fairs.

Food Scientist

There are around 7.7 billion people on Earth. That number grows every day. That's a lot of mouths to feed! Food scientists help meet that need. They find ways that farmers can grow more crops and raise healthier animals. They also find ways to make better processed foods. These are foods that are made from other foods. Some examples are pasta, breads, and cereals.

Food scientists test different kinds of soil, fertilizer, and light sources to see which ones grow the best fruits and vegetables.

On the Job

Food scientists work in **laboratories** and offices. They do experiments. They also work in fields and on farms. Food scientists study plant and animal food sources. They often go to where these sources live and grow. The scientists take soil samples to see if **nutrients** are missing. They study animals and find ways to make meat, milk, egg, and poultry production better. They also show farmers ways to control weeds and pests.

Pay Range

Average salary = $64,000 per year.

Education and Skills

Most food scientists have a four-year college degree. They study food science, chemistry, or biology. Many food scientists get master's or doctorate degrees in food science. Food scientists are always learning. They must have computer skills and be able to work with lab tools.

Taste Tester

Do you have a favorite cookie or ice cream? It is probably your favorite because it tastes so good. But what if the flavor changed every time you ate it? That is not likely to happen thanks to taste testers.

On the Job

Taste testers work for food companies. They spend their days tasting small bites of food. They make sure a product has a good flavor. They pay attention to how the food feels. They take several bites of the same food item. In between bites, they drink water to clear the flavor from their mouth. Taste testers even smell the food. Some taste testers try out new flavors of ice cream or breakfast cereal. Others make sure a company's regular products meet certain standards. Taste testers can work full-time for a large company. Or they can work part-time testing new foods.

FUN FACT

Some taste testers have top secret government clearance! These special tasters work for presidents and world leaders. They check for ingredients that might cause allergies and make sure the food is to the leader's liking.

Pay Range

Between $24,000 and $42,000 per year.

Education and Skills

Taste testers do not have to go to college. Some have degrees in food science. Others learn on the job. They must be willing to try many new foods. Good taste testers care for their taste buds. This means they eat a healthy diet and drink lots of water. They avoid salty and spicy foods. This helps their taste buds stay open to new tastes. A taste tester must be able to tell how sweet, salty, bitter, or acidic foods are. Taste testers have to be good at writing and speaking. They must be able to describe the foods they taste.

Some taste testers get to try bites of cakes and pies all day!

Glossary

agriculture (AG-rih-kul-chur)—the science of growing crops

apprentice (uh-PREN-tiss)—someone who learns a job by working with a skilled person

catering (KAY-tur-ing)—providing and serving food

culinary (KUHL-ih-nare-ee)—related to cooking or the kitchen

edible (ED-uh-buhl)—able to be eaten

entrepreneur (ahn-truh-pruh-NOO-er)—a person who starts his or her own business

internship (IN-turn-ship)—a temporary job in which a person works with and learns from experienced workers

laboratory (LA-bruh-tor-ree)—a room where scientists do experiments and tests

nutrient (NOO-tree-uhnt)—a part of food, like a vitamin, that is used to help the body grow

portfolio (port-FOH-lee-oh)—an album of pictures used to show clients a photographer's experience

profit (PROF-it)—money that a business makes after expenses have been paid

Read More

America's Test Kitchen. *The Complete Cookbook for Young Chefs.* Naperville, IL: Sourcebooks Jabberwocky, 2018.

Brisson, Pat. *Before We Eat: From Farm to Table.* Thomaston, ME: Tilbury House Publishers, 2018.

Huff, Lisa. *Kid Chef Bakes: The Kids Cookbook for Aspiring Bakers.* Berkeley, CA: Rockridge Press, 2017.

Phillips, Tanya. *Beginning Beekeeping: Everything You Need to Make Your Hive Thrive!* Indianapolis, IN: DK Publishing, 2017.

Internet Sites

Food Foraging for Kids
https://wilderchild.com/foraging-for-wild-edibles-with-kids/

Food Truck
https://pbskids.org/lunchlab/games/food-truck

My American Farm
http://www.myamericanfarm.org/

Recipes Kids Can Bake
https://www.foodnetwork.com/recipes/packages/recipes-for-kids/weekends-at-home/recipes-kids-can-bake

Index